Mortimer's Math

Counting

Karen Bryant-Mole

Gareth Stevens Publishing
MILWAUKEE

Mortimer's Math

For a free color catalog describing Gareth Stevens' list of high-quality books and multimedia programs, call 1-800-542-2595 (USA) or 1-800-461-9120 (Canada). Gareth Stevens Publishing's Fax: (414) 225-0377.

Library of Congress Cataloging-in-Publication Data available upon request from publisher. Fax: (414) 225-0377 for the attention of the Publishing Records Department.

ISBN 0-8368-2617-5

This North American edition first published in 2000 by
Gareth Stevens Publishing
1555 North RiverCenter Drive, Suite 201
Milwaukee, WI 53212 USA

Created by Karen Bryant-Mole
Photographs by Zul Mukhida
Designed by Jean Wheeler
Teddy bear by Merrythought Ltd.

Printed in the United States of America

1 2 3 4 5 6 7 8 9 04 03 02 01 00

contents

Mortimer the bear is wearing one party hat.

1

one balloon

one slice of
birthday cake

How many presents
can you count?

Mortimer has
two boots.

1, 2

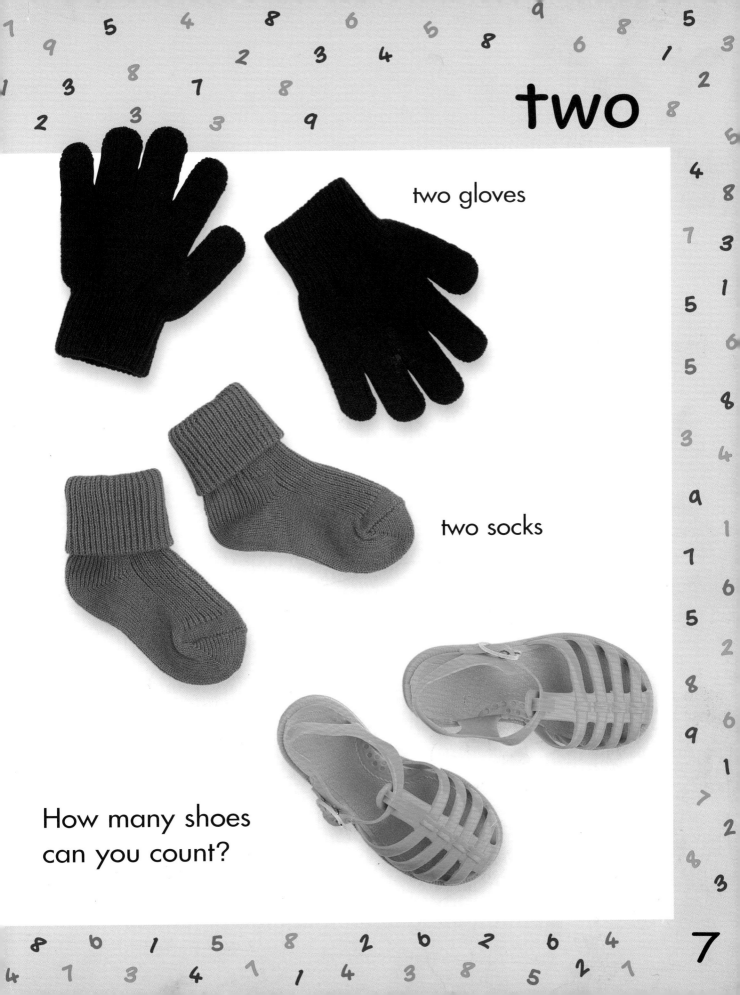

two gloves

two socks

How many shoes
can you count?

3

Mortimer is playing with three cars.

1, 2, 3

three

three boats

three tractors

FARM MOTOR

How many
train engines
can you count?

four

four markers

four crayons

How many
pencils can
you count?

Mortimer has five plates.

five

five cups

How many saucers can you count?

six buckets

How many shovels can you count?

7

Mortimer bought seven apples at the store.

1, 2, 3, 4, 5, 6, 7

seven

seven oranges

How many pears can you count?

8

Mortimer is playing with eight tiger cubs.

1, 2, 3, 4, 5, 6, 7, 8

eight

eight giraffes

How many
elephants can
you count?

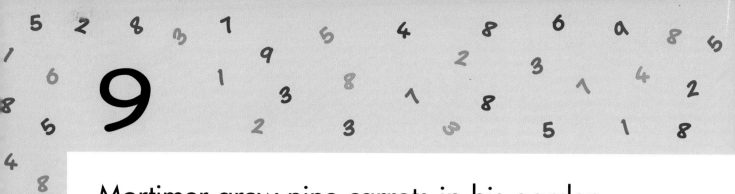

Mortimer grew nine carrots in his garden.

nine potatoes

How many tomatoes can you count?

Mortimer has ten colorful spoons.

1, 2, 3, 4, 5, 6, 7, 8, 9, 10

ten knives

How many forks
can you count?

glossary/index

bucket — a deep container with a curved handle used to carry things, such as sand or water; a pail 15

cubs — young lions, tigers, wolves, or bears 18

engine — the part of a train that is used to pull or push railroad cars along a track 9

party — a group of people gathered together to celebrate an occasion or just to have fun 4

present — a gift 5

saucers — small, flat dishes that are placed underneath cups 13

shovel — a tool with a handle and a flattened scoop used for digging 15

slice — a thin, flat piece cut from something larger, like a cake or a loaf of bread 5

videos

123 Count With Me. (Children's Television Workshop)

Blue's Clues: ABCs and 123s. (Viacom International)

Count With Maisy. (Polygram Visual Programming)

Richard Scarry's Best Counting Video. (Random House)